American Songwriters SERIES

George & Ira Gershwin

Contents

12 Bess, You Is My Woman Now

 4 Bidin' My Time

20 But Not for Me

38 Embraceable You

28 Fascinating Rhythm

24 A Foggy Day

 8 I Got Rhythm

46 I Loves You, Porgy

52 I've Got a Crush On You

56 It Ain't Necessarily So

62 Let's Call the Whole Thing Off

68 Love Is Here to Stay

72 The Man I Love

32 Nice Work If You Can Get It

42 Of Thee I Sing (Baby)

76 Oh, Lady Be Good!

80 'S Wonderful

92 Someone to Watch Over Me

84 Summertime

88 They Can't Take That Away From Me

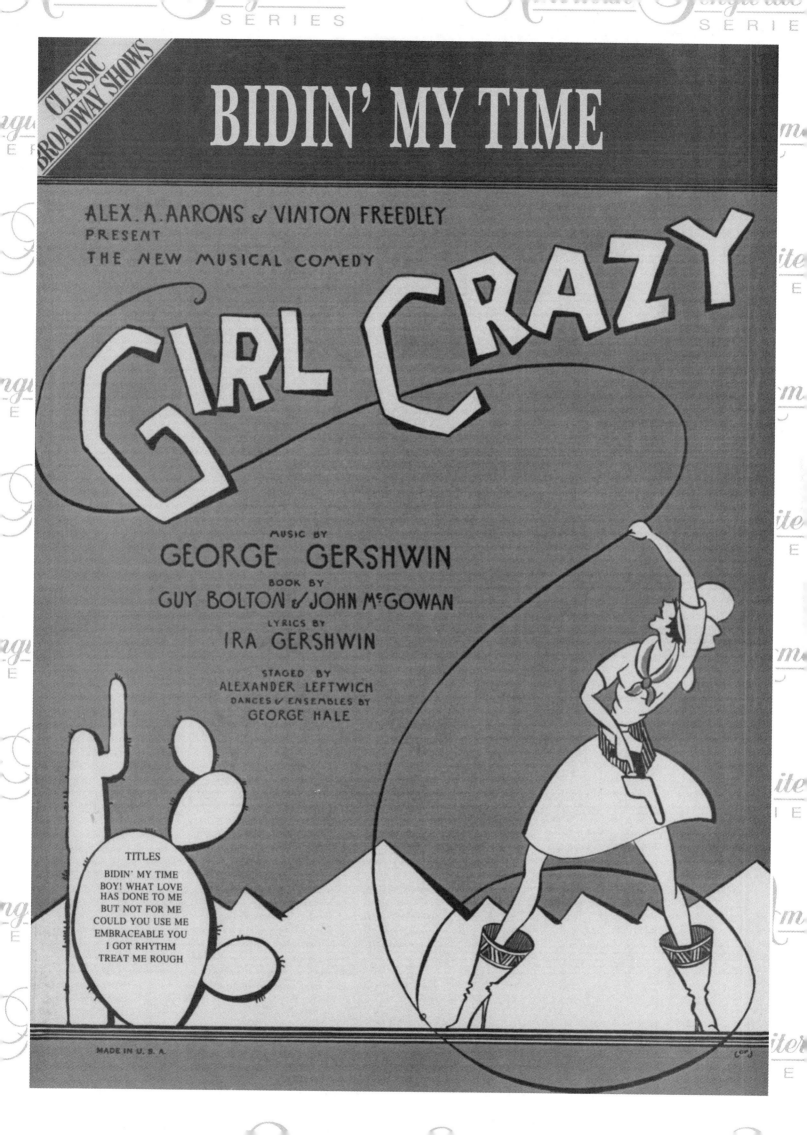

BIDIN' MY TIME

Music and Lyrics by
GEORGE GERSHWIN
and IRA GERSHWIN

Moderato

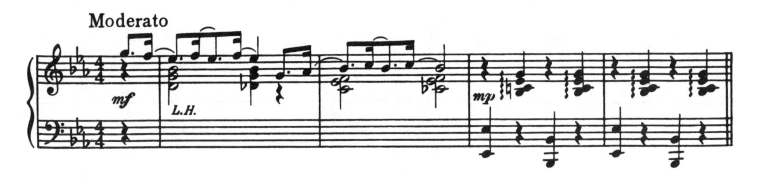

Gracefully

Some fel-lers love to Tip-Toe Through The Tu-lips;___
Some fel-lers love to Tell It To The Dai-sies;___

Some fel-lers go on Sing - - ing In The Rain.___
Some Stroll Be-neath The Hon - ey-suc-kle Vines;___

Bidin' My Time - 3 - 1

6

I GOT RHYTHM

Music and Lyrics by
GEORGE GERSHWIN
and IRA GERSHWIN

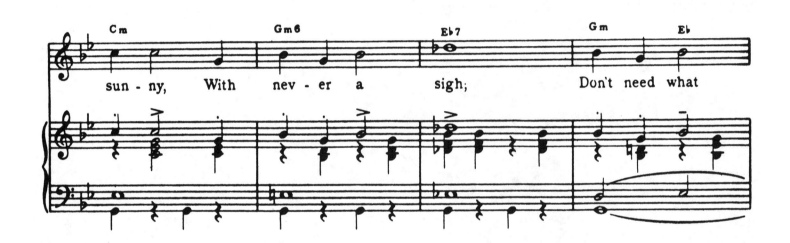

I Got Rhythm - 4 - 1

BESS, YOU IS MY WOMAN NOW

By
GEORGE GERSHWIN,
DuBOSE and DOROTHY HEYWARD
and IRA GERSHWIN

Bess, You Is My Woman Now - 8 - 1

BUT NOT FOR ME

Music and Lyrics by
GEORGE GERSHWIN
and IRA GERSHWIN

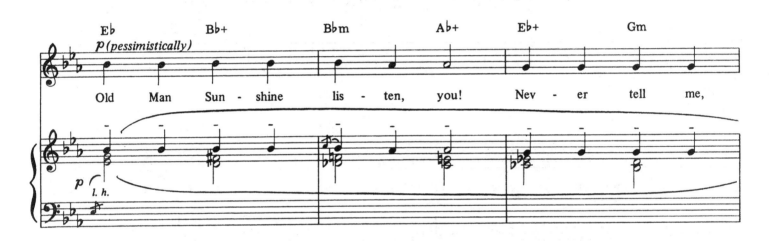

Old Man Sun - shine lis - ten, you! Nev - er tell me,

"Dreams come true!" Just try it And I'll start a ri - ot.

But Not for Me - 4 - 1

A FOGGY DAY

Music and Lyrics by
GEORGE GERSHWIN
and IRA GERSHWIN

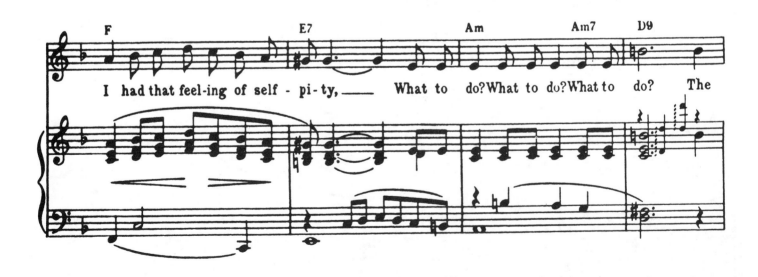

A Foggy Day - 4 - 1

A Foggy Day - 4 - 4

FASCINATING RHYTHM

Music and Lyrics by
GEORGE GERSHWIN
and IRA GERSHWIN

Moderato

Got a lit-tle rhy-thm, A rhy-thm, a rhy-thm That pit-a-pats through my brain. So darn per-sis-tent, The day is-n't dis-tant When it-'ll drive me in-sane. Comes in the morn-ing With-

Fascinating Rhythm - 4 - 1

out an-y warn-ing, And hangs a-round all day. I'll have to sneak up to it,

Some-day, and speak up to it, I hope it list-ens when I say:

REFRAIN

"Fas-ci-nat-ing Rhy-thm You've got me on the go! Fas-ci-nat-ing Rhy-thm I'm all a-

qui-ver. What a mess you're mak-ing! The neigh-bors want to know why I'm

NICE WORK IF YOU CAN GET IT

Music and Lyrics by
GEORGE GERSHWIN
and IRA GERSHWIN

The man who on-ly lives for mak-ing mon-ey Lives a life that is-n't nec-es-sa-ri-ly sun-ny. Like-wise the man who works for fame,

34

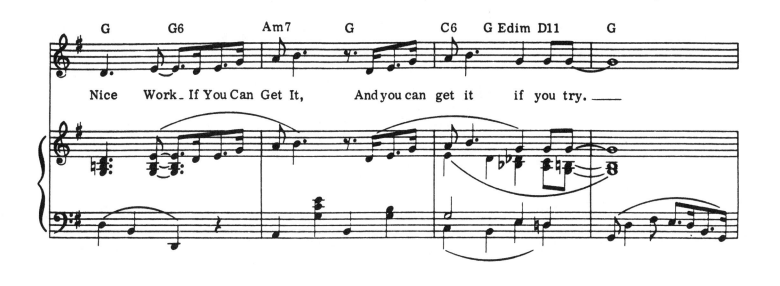

Nice Work — If You Can Get It, And you can get it if you try. ___

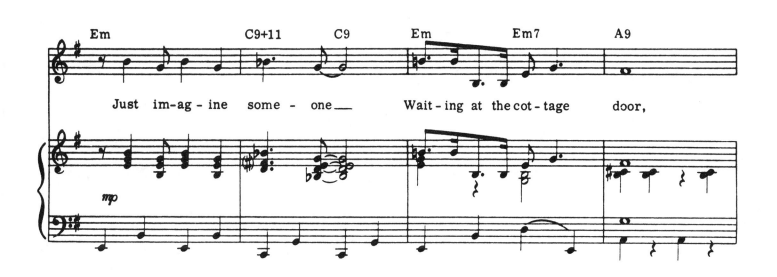

Just im-ag-ine some - one ___ Wait-ing at the cot-tage door,

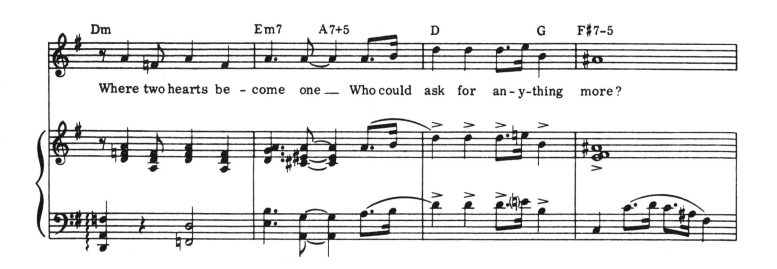

Where two hearts be - come one ___ Who could ask for an-y-thing more?

EMBRACEABLE YOU

Music by GEORGE GERSHWIN

Words by IRA GERSHWIN

What a joy to see.. M·G·M's Musical!

An American in Paris

TO THE MUSIC OF
George GERSHWIN

starring
Gene KELLY

and introducing
Leslie CARON

Oscar LEVANT

Georges GUETARY

Nina FOCH

Technicolor

Alan Jay Lerner

Arthur Freed

Vincente Minnelli

A METRO-GOLDWYN-MAYER PICTURE

TRA-LA-LA

'S WONDERFUL

I GOT RHYTHM

EMBRACEABLE YOU

I'LL BUILD A STAIRWAY
TO PARADISE

Printed in U.S.A.

Price
60¢
in U.S.A.

EMBRACEABLE YOU

Music and Lyrics by
GEORGE GERSHWIN
and IRA GERSHWIN

What was it that con-trolled_ me? What kept my love-life lean?
My nose I used to turn _ up When you'd be-siege my heart;

My in-tu-i-tion told _ me You'd come on the scene. La - dy,
Now I com-plete-ly burn _ up When you're slow to start. I'm a-

lis-ten to the rhy-thm of my heart-beat, And you'll get just what I mean.
fraid you'll have to take the con-se-quenc-es, You up - set the ap-ple cart.

rall. e dim.

OF THEE I SING
(Baby)

Music and Lyrics by
GEORGE GERSHWIN
and IRA GERSHWIN

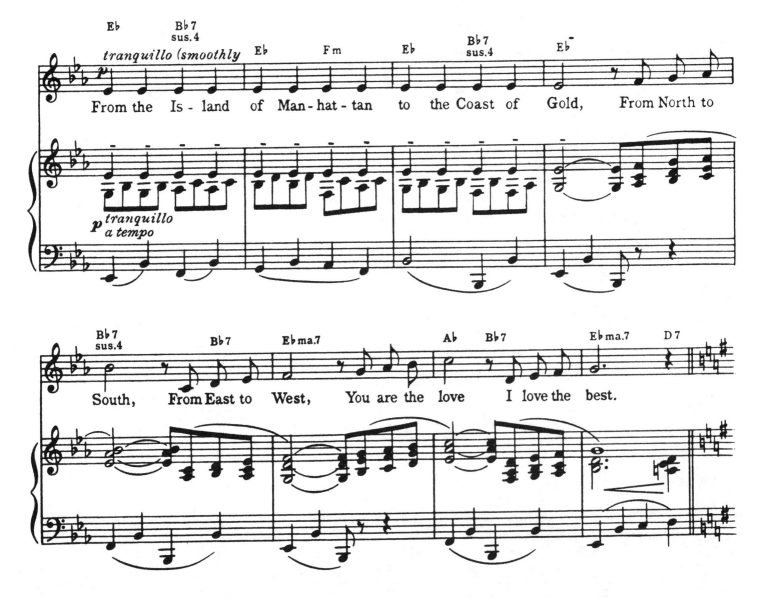

I LOVES YOU, PORGY

By
GEORGE GERSHWIN,
DuBOSE and DOROTHY HEYWARD
and IRA GERSHWIN

Allegretto (With strength and rhythm)

I'VE GOT A CRUSH ON YOU

EDGAR SELWYN PRESENTS

CLARK & McCULLOUGH

IN

STRIKE UP THE BAND

TITLES

HANGIN' AROUND WITH YOU
I MEAN TO SAY
I WANT TO BE A WAR BRIDE
I'VE GOT A CRUSH ON YOU
MADEMOISELLE IN NEW ROCHELLE
THE MAN I LOVE
MILITARY DANCING DRILL
SOON
STRIKE UP THE BAND

MUSIC BY
GEORGE GERSHWIN

LYRICS BY
IRA GERSHWIN

BOOK BY
MORRIE RYSKIND
BASED ON THE LIBRETTO BY GEORGE S. KAUFMAN

STAGED BY
ALEXANDER LEFTWICH
DANCES & ENSEMBLES BY
GEORGE HALE

MADE IN U. S. A.

I'VE GOT A CRUSH ON YOU

Music and Lyrics by
GEORGE GERSHWIN
and IRA GERSHWIN

Allegretto giocoso *(gayly)*

He: How
She: How

glad the man-y mil-lions of An-na-belles and Lill-ians would be_____
glad a mil-lion lad-dies from mill-ion-aires to cad-dies would be_____

___ to cap-ture me! _____ But you had such per-sist-ence, you

I've Got a Crush on You - 4 - 1

wore down my re-sist-ance: I fell, _____ and it was swell. _____

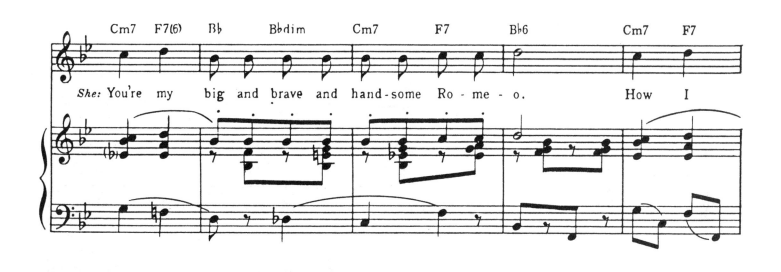

She: You're my big and brave and hand-some Ro - me - o. How I

won you I shall nev-er, nev-er know. *He:* It's not that you're at - trac-tive, But

IT AIN'T NECESSARILY SO

By
GEORGE GERSHWIN,
DuBOSE and DOROTHY HEYWARD
and IRA GERSHWIN

It Ain't Necessarily So - 6 - 1

LET'S CALL THE WHOLE THING OFF

Music and Lyrics by
GEORGE GERSHWIN
and IRA GERSHWIN

Let's Call the Whole Thing Off - 6 - 1

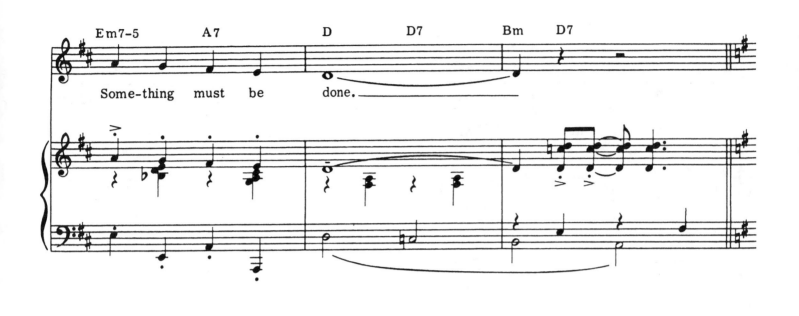

Off!

66

LOVE IS HERE TO STAY

Music and Lyrics by
GEORGE GERSHWIN
and IRA GERSHWIN

The more I read the pa-pers The less I com-pre-hend The

world and all its ca-pers And how it all will end. Noth-ing seems to be

Love Is Here to Stay - 4 - 1

THE MAN I LOVE

Music and Lyrics by
GEORGE GERSHWIN
and IRA GERSHWIN

When the mel-low moon be-gins to beam, ev-'ry night I dream a lit-tle dream,

and, of course, Prince Charm-ing is the theme, the he for me. Al-

The Man I Love - 4 - 1

The Man I Love - 4 - 2

75

The Man I Love - 4 - 4

OH, LADY BE GOOD!

Music and Lyrics by
GEORGE GERSHWIN
and IRA GERSHWIN

Lis - ten to my tale of woe, It's ter - ri - bly sad, but true.
Au - burn and bru - nette and blonde, I love 'em all, tall or small.

All dressed up, no place to go, Each ev - 'ning I'm aw - f'ly blue.
But some - how they don't grow fond, They stag - ger but nev - er fall.

I must win some win - some miss; Can't go on like this.
Win - ter's gone, and now it's Spring! Love! where is thy sting?

Oh, Lady Be Good! - 3 - 1

'S WONDERFUL
Music and Lyrics by GEORGE and IRA GERSHWIN
'S WONDERFUL
FUNNY FACE
Price
60¢
in U.S.A.
From the Paramount Picture
AUDREY HEPBURN and FRED ASTAIRE
in
FUNNY FACE
co-starring KAY THOMPSON
with Michel Auclair · Robert Flemyng · Choreography by Eugene Loring and Fred Astaire · Music and Lyrics by George and Ira Gershwin
Additional music and lyrics by Roger Edens and Leonard Gershe · Produced by Roger Edens
Directed by Stanley Donen · Written by Leonard Gershe · Songs staged by Stanley Donen
WHEN PERFORMING THIS COMPOSITION KINDLY GIVE ALL PROGRAM CREDITS TO
TECHNICOLOR
VISTAVISION
NEW WORLD MUSIC CORP.
NEW YORK, N. Y.
PRINTED IN U.S.A.

'S WONDERFUL

Music and Lyrics by
GEORGE GERSHWIN
and IRA GERSHWIN

'S Wonderful - 4 - 4

SUMMERTIME

By
GEORGE GERSHWIN,
DuBOSE and DOROTHY HEYWARD
and IRA GERSHWIN

Sum - mer time _____ an' the liv - in' is

Summertime - 4 - 1

THEY CAN'T TAKE THAT AWAY FROM ME

Music and Lyrics by
GEORGE GERSHWIN
and IRA GERSHWIN

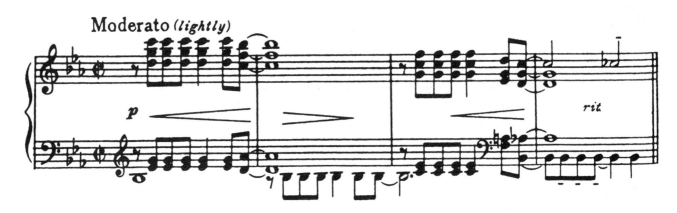

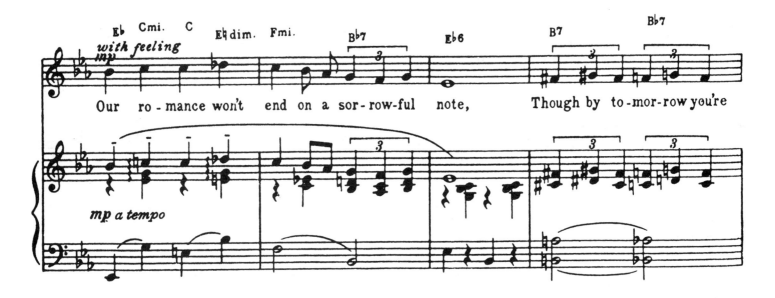

Our ro-mance won't end on a sor-row-ful note, Though by to-mor-row you're

gone;___ The song is end-ed, but as the song-writ-er wrote, The

They Can't Take That Away From Me - 4 - 1

90

SOMEONE TO WATCH OVER ME

Music and Lyrics by
GEORGE GERSHWIN
and IRA GERSHWIN

Someone to Watch Over Me - 4 - 1

Look - ing ev - 'ry-where, have - n't found him yet; he's the big af - fair I can-

not for-get. On - ly man I ev - er think of with re - gret.

I'd like to add his i - ni - tial to my mon - o - gram.

Tell me, where is the shep-herd for this lost lamb?